Butterflies and Moths

Words by Dean Morris

Raintree Childrens Books
Milwaukee • Toronto • Melbourne • London

Library of Congress Number: 77-7912

6 7 8 9 0 86 85 84

Printed and bound in the United States of America.

Library of Congress Cataloging in Publication Data

Morris, Dean.
    Butterflies and moths.

    (Read about)
    Includes index.
    SUMMARY: Discusses the life cycles and behavior
patterns of various species of butterflies and
moths.
    1. Lepidoptera — Juvenile literature.
[1. Butterflies. 2. Moths]   I.   Title.
QL544.2.M67   595.7'8   77-7912
ISBN 0-8393-0010-7 lib. bdg.

This book has been reviewed
for accuracy by

Carl W. Albrecht
Curator of Natural History
The Ohio Historical Society

Butterflies
and Moths

tortoiseshell butterfly

monarch butterfly

tiger moth

red admiral butterfly

common blue butterfly

purple emperor butterfly

cabbage butterfly

Butterflies and moths are alike in many ways. They belong to the same group of insects. They have lovely markings and colors on their wings.

Butterflies and moths are different in some ways too. Most butterflies like to fly in the daytime. They like the sun. They rest on cloudy days.

hawk
moth

hawk
moth

goat moth

Most moths fly at night. They often fly toward the light.

Another way to tell most moths and butterflies apart is to look at them when they are resting. Moths usually rest with their wings open. Butterflies often rest with their wings closed.

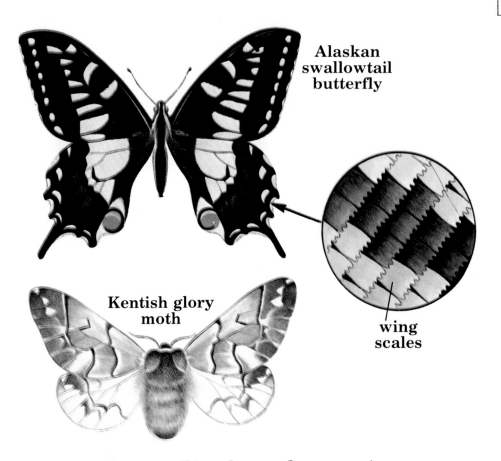

Alaskan swallowtail butterfly

Kentish glory moth

wing scales

Most butterflies have large wings. They have thin bodies. Moths usually have smaller wings, but larger bodies.

The wings of moths and butterflies are covered with tiny scales. Each scale is colored. There are thousands of scales on each wing.

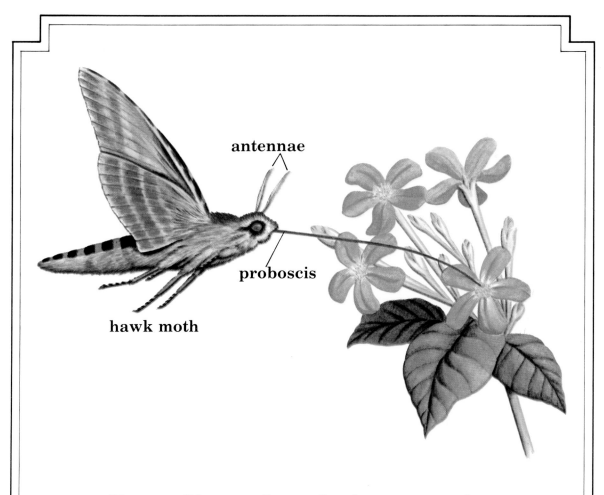

antennae

proboscis

hawk moth

    Butterflies and moths have very long tongues. The tongue is hollow, like a straw. It is called a proboscis. Moths and butterflies suck the juices from flowers through their proboscises.

    Butterflies and moths smell with their antennae. They can taste with their feet.

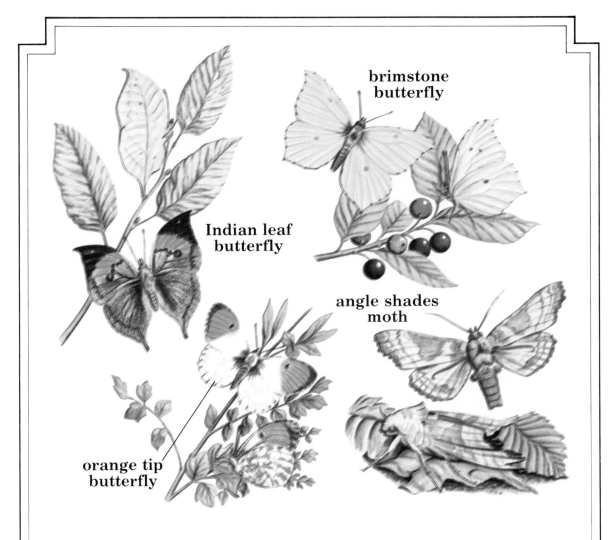

brimstone
butterfly

Indian leaf
butterfly

angle shades
moth

orange tip
butterfly

Why are butterflies and moths so many different colors? One reason is that they live in many different kinds of places. Often moths and butterflies are the same color or colors as the plants among

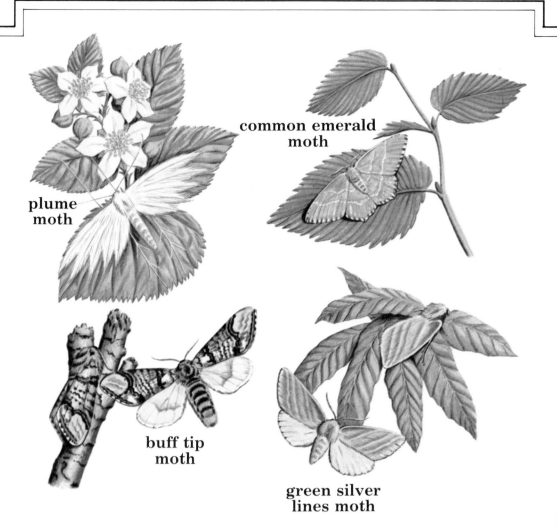

plume
moth

common emerald
moth

buff tip
moth

green silver
lines moth

which they live.

Their colors protect them. It is hard
for birds and other enemies to see them.

Can you find the moths and butterflies
on these pages?

Some moths and butterflies adapt, or change, and are protected.

These are peppered moths. Not long ago, most of these moths were light in color. Most of the trees where they lived were light too. Then people made factories nearby. Smoke from the factories made the trees dirty and black. Birds could see the light moths on the dark trees. So the light moths began to die out. Now there are more dark moths than light moths where the trees are dark.

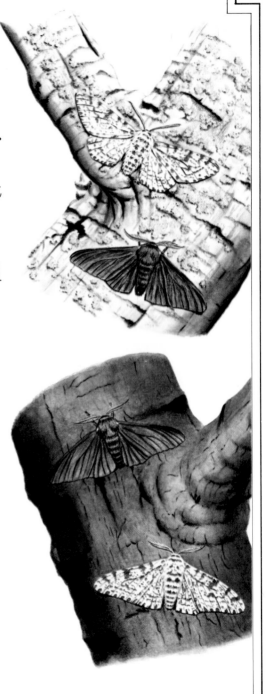

bee hawk moth

bumblebee

Butterflies and moths are protected in other ways too. Some look like other insects.

This moth looks like a bee. Its wings make a buzzing sound like a bee. Birds know that bees can sting. So they stay away from the moth.

Some moths have large spots on their wings. The spots look like eyes. If something bothers the moth, it shakes its wings and scares the enemy away.

eyed hawk moth

This butterfly has a false head on its back wings. If a bird attacks the false head, the butterfly can still get away safely.

false-headed butterfly

Not all moths can fly. Some female moths crawl on trees or bushes. They have a special smell so that the male moths know where they are.

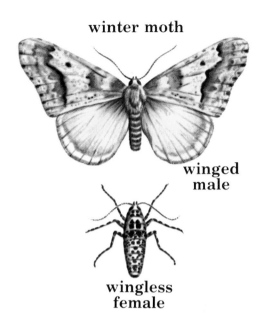

winter moth

winged male

wingless female

Apollo butterfly

Butterflies and most moths can fly. They live in places all over the world. Most butterflies live in warm places. But some live in cold places, even high up in the mountains.

**painted lady
butterfly**

Some butterflies fly on very long
trips. This is a painted lady butterfly.
It flies across land and over water.
Monarch butterflies live in North
America in the summer. They fly to Mexico

monarch
butterflies

and southern California where it is warm in
wintertime. In the spring, the monarchs fly
back north again. They lay their eggs on
the way. Moving with the seasons like this
is called migration.

cabbage
butterfly

egg

Butterflies and moths change shape and form several times during their lives.

They start life as tiny eggs. The female lays the eggs.

caterpillars

Most eggs are laid on leaves. A caterpillar comes out of each egg. The caterpillars eat the leaves. They eat much of the time and grow very fast.

Caterpillars' skins do not stretch very much. They change their skins as they grow. We call this molting. One caterpillar has several different skins. When a caterpillar is ready to change its old skin, the old skin splits. Then the caterpillar crawls out of its old skin.

When the caterpillar is fully grown, it turns into a pupa. The pupa case hangs onto a leaf by fine silky threads.

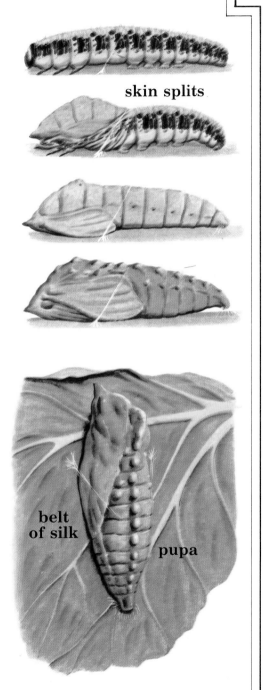

skin splits

belt of silk

pupa

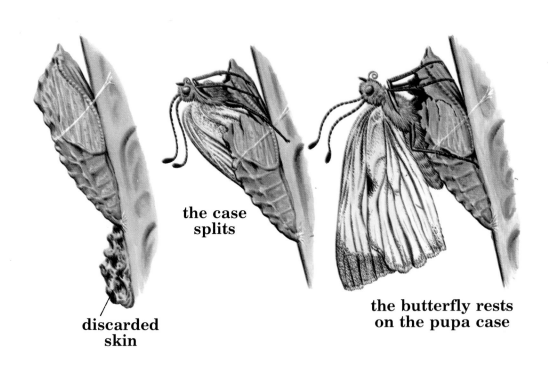

the case
splits

discarded
skin

the butterfly rests
on the pupa case

Inside the case, the pupa changes into a butterfly or moth.

When the butterfly is ready to come out, the case breaks. The new butterfly's wings are wet and sticky. The butterfly rests on the empty pupa case. Its wings stretch and dry in the sun.

Some butterflies live
for only a few weeks. They
fly away and find mates.
Then they lay eggs and the
story begins again.

eggs

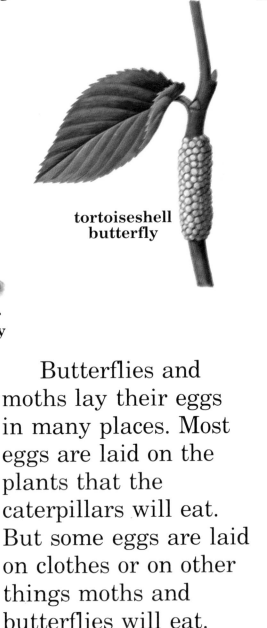

clothes moth

tortoiseshell
butterfly

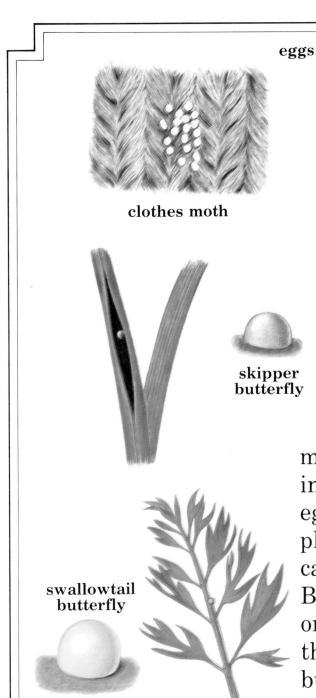

skipper
butterfly

swallowtail
butterfly

Butterflies and moths lay their eggs in many places. Most eggs are laid on the plants that the caterpillars will eat. But some eggs are laid on clothes or on other things moths and butterflies will eat.

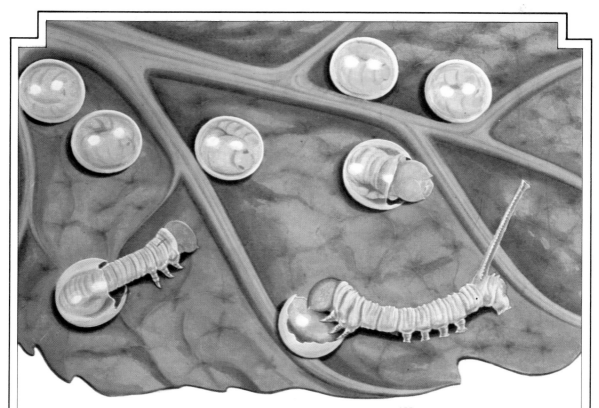

**caterpillar eats
remains of egg**

The eggs are very small. A tiny
caterpillar grows inside each egg. The
caterpillars make holes in the shells of
their eggs. Then they can come out, or
hatch. Often the young caterpillars eat
what is left of the eggs.

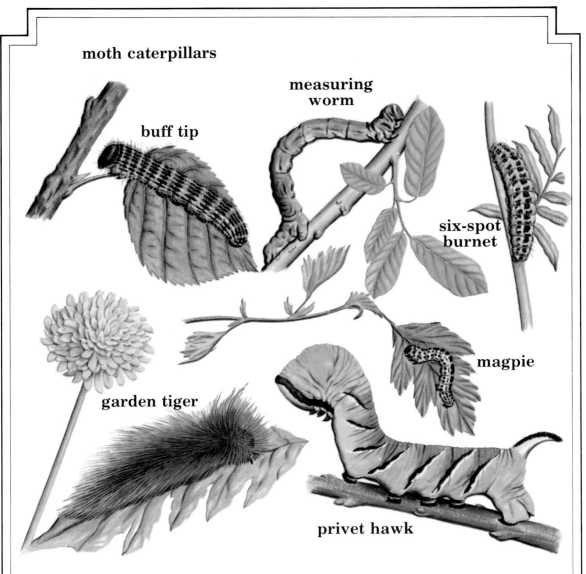

moth caterpillars

measuring worm

buff tip

six-spot burnet

magpie

garden tiger

privet hawk

There are many different shapes, colors, and sizes of caterpillars. These are the caterpillars of some moths. Did you ever see some of them where you live?

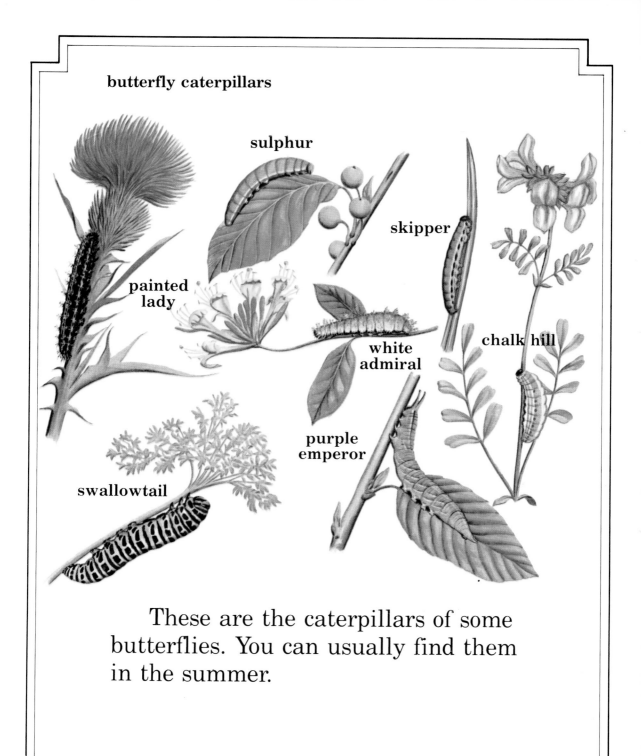

butterfly caterpillars

sulphur

painted lady

skipper

chalk hill

white admiral

purple emperor

swallowtail

These are the caterpillars of some butterflies. You can usually find them in the summer.

moth caterpillars

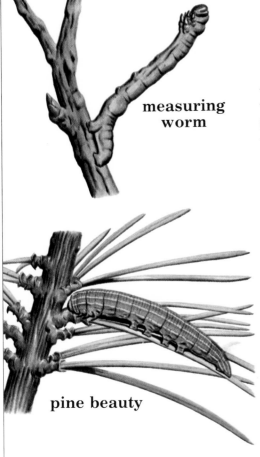

measuring
worm

pine beauty

Caterpillars are protected in some of the same ways as moths and butterflies.

Some caterpillars look like parts of the plants on which they live. Birds cannot see them very well.

Other caterpillars have a bad taste. Their bright colors warn birds not to attack them.

cinnabar

caterpillars

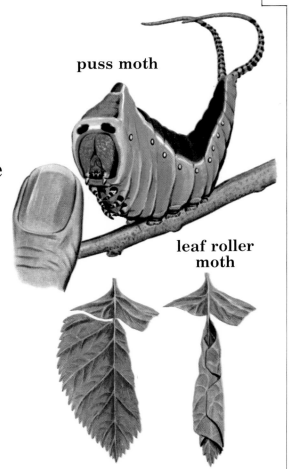

puss moth

leaf roller
moth

The puss moth caterpillar scares birds away. It has a false face and two tails. It also squirts acid at birds.

The leaf roller rolls itself up inside a leaf. Birds cannot see it.

Some caterpillars have spots on their bodies that scare birds away. This caterpillar looks like a snake.

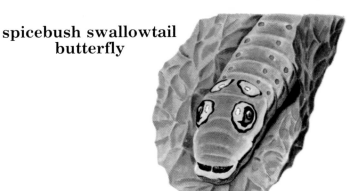

spicebush swallowtail
butterfly

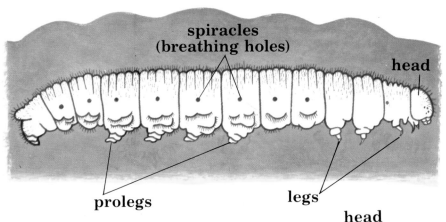

spiracles
(breathing holes)

head

prolegs

legs

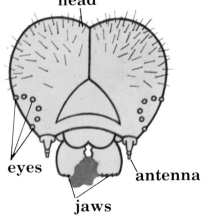

head

eyes

jaws

antenna

A caterpillar's body has thirteen parts behind the head. The last two are close together. There are tiny holes on some of the parts. These holes are called spiracles. A caterpillar breathes through the spiracles.

A caterpillar usually has six eyes on each side of its head. But it cannot see very well. Caterpillars feel with their antennae. They have strong jaws that help them eat.

moth caterpillars

clothes

codling

leaf miner

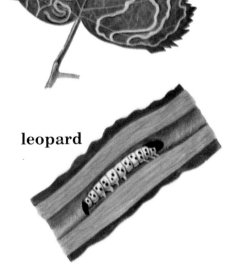

Most caterpillars eat leaves. But the codling moth caterpillar eats fruit. The clothes moth caterpillar eats wool. The leaf miner caterpillar eats its way inside a leaf. The leopard moth caterpillar lives inside plant stems.

leopard

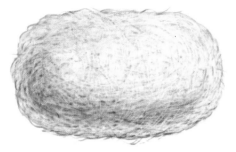

cocoon of
silken threads

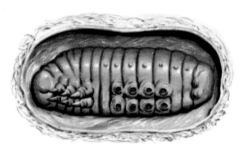

Many moth caterpillars make cocoons. A cocoon is a kind of coat around the caterpillar. From the outside, the cocoon looks like a furry ball.

Inside the cocoon a lot is going on. The caterpillar changes into a pupa. Then the pupa changes into a moth.

The moth does not come out of the cocoon until the weather is warm enough.

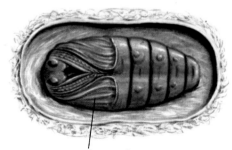

the wings
are formed

Moth cocoons are
made of tiny threads.
The caterpillars spin
the thread themselves.

cocoon

hawk moth pupa

Some moth
caterpillars do not
make cocoons.
They dig holes for
themselves instead.

This caterpillar
hides itself inside a
hollow plant stem.

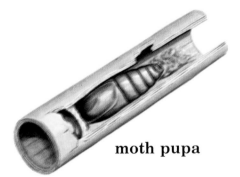

moth pupa

The caterpillar of the china mark moth lives under the water. It lives in a bag that it makes for itself. The bag is made of silk and bits of waterweed. The caterpillar eats waterweed. The caterpillar spins a cocoon inside its bag. After the pupa turns into a moth, the moth swims to the top of the water.

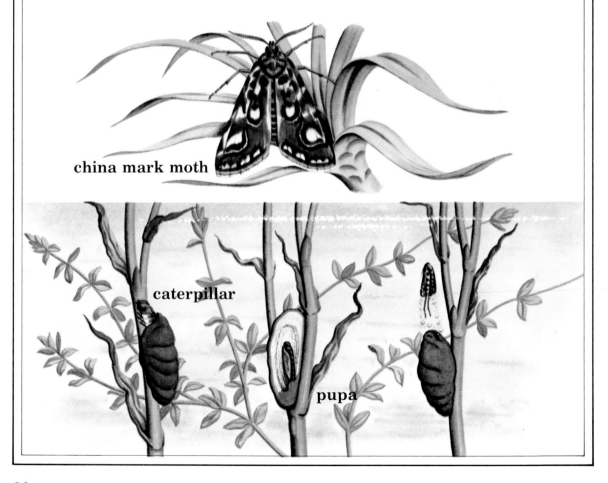

china mark moth

caterpillar

pupa

large blue butterfly

The caterpillars of the large blue butterfly eat leaves until they are through growing. Then they fall to the ground. Ants find the caterpillars. The caterpillars make a sweet juice that the ants like to drink. The ants carry the caterpillars back to their nest. In the nest, larvae are hatching from ant eggs. The larvae look like tiny worms. The caterpillars eat the ant larvae. They stay in the ant nest until they turn into butterflies. Then they crawl out and fly away.

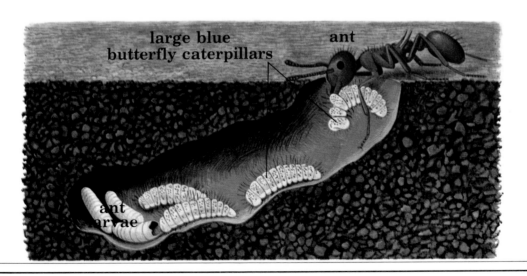
large blue butterfly caterpillars
ant
ant larvae

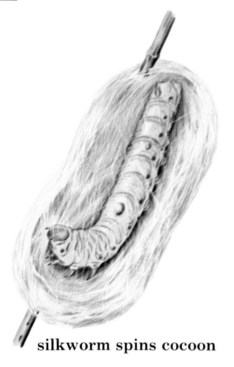

silkworm spins cocoon

Silk moth caterpillars are called silkworms. Silkworms eat the leaves of mulberry bushes. They make thick cocoons of silk. People gather the cocoons. They make silk thread out of them.

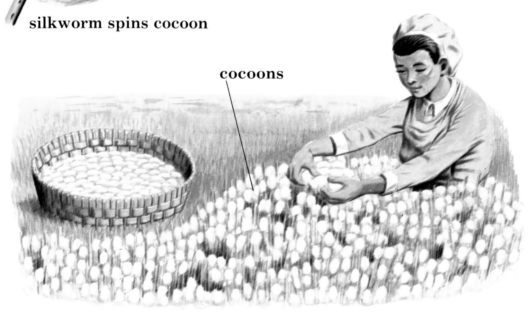

cocoons

People drop the cocoons into boiling water. This kills the silkworms inside. The heat makes the silk loose. People can then take the silk thread off the cocoons and wind it onto spools.

Silkworm threads are very fine. But many threads can be twisted together. That makes a thicker thread. It is strong enough to make into cloth. Silk is the finest cloth in the world.

Collecting

First, you will need to buy a butterfly net from your neighborhood hobby store. Or, if you like, you can make one from a seven-foot length of branch. To do this, loop the springy end around in a fifteen-inch hoop and fasten it tightly to the lower section with heavy string. Then fasten a bag of fine netting to this frame. Ask an adult to help you.

You will also need a large-mouth jar with a lid, some cotton, and a piece of paper. Place the cotton in the bottom of the jar. Ask an adult to add some ammonia to the cotton. Then cover the cotton with a round piece of paper. The paper will protect the butterfly's wings from damage. Close the jar tightly. Keep it closed until you are ready to put a butterfly inside.

Drying

Make a mounting board by gluing three pieces of wood or Styrofoam together. Leave an opening in the center. Place the butterfly's body over the center opening. Hold the wings in place with strips of paper and long pins. Let the wings dry completely before mounting.

Mounting

Find several flat boxes. Place some smooth, flat cotton in the bottom of each one. Put several mothballs under the cotton to protect your collection from pests that might eat them. Place your butterflies and moths on top of the cotton. Label each butterfly or moth with its scientific name, the date it was captured, and the place you found it. Cover the box tightly with plastic wrapping and tape.

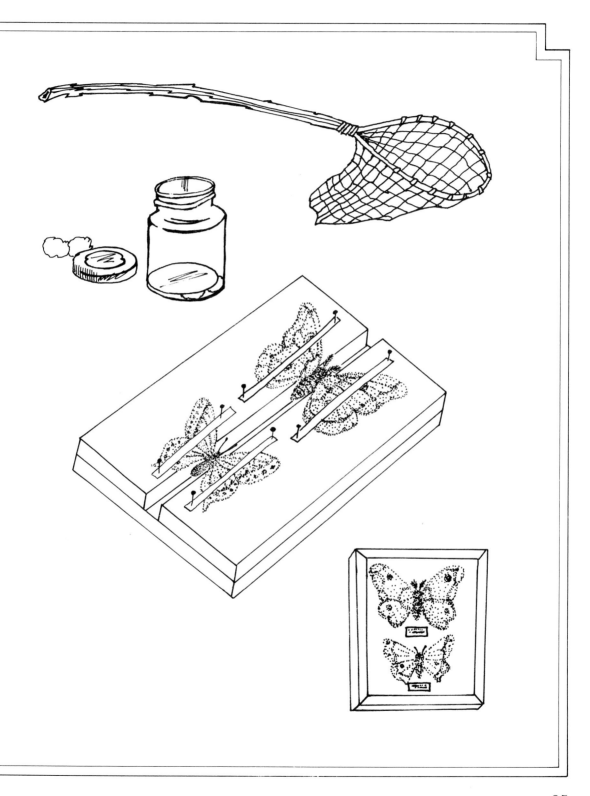

Where to Read About the Butterflies and Moths

common emerald moth (kom′ ən em′ ər əld
  môth) *p. 9*
eyed hawk moth (īd hôk môth) *p. 12*
false-headed butterfly (fôls hed′əd
  but′ ər flī′) *p. 12*
garden tiger moth (gärd′ ən tī′ gər môth)
  p. 22
goat moth (gōt môth) *p. 5*
green silver lines moth (grēn sil′ vər
  līnz môth) *p. 9*
hawk moth (hôk môth) *pp. 5, 7, 29*
Indian leaf butterfly (in′ dē ən lēf
  but′ ər flī′) *p. 8*
Kentish glory moth (kent′ ish glôr′ ē môth)
  p. 6
large blue butterfly (lärj bloo but′ ər flī′)
  p. 31
leaf miner (lēf mīn′ ər) *p. 27*
leaf roller (lēf rō′ lər) *p. 25*
leopard moth (lēp ərd môth) *p. 27*
magpie moth (mag′ pī môth) *p. 22*

measuring worm (mezh′ ər ing wurm)
  pp. 22, 24
monarch butterfly (mon′ ərk but′ ər flī′)
  pp. 4, 15
orange tip butterfly (ôr′ inj tip
  but′ ər flī′) *p. 8*
painted lady butterfly (pānt′ id lā′ dē
  but′ ər flī′) *pp. 14, 23*
peppered moth (pep′ ərd môth) *p. 10*
pine beauty moth (pīn byoo′ tē môth) *p. 24*
plume moth (ploom môth) *p. 9*
privet hawk moth (priv′ ət hôk môth) *p. 22*
purple emperor butterfly (pur′ pəl em′ pər ər
  but′ ər flī′) *pp. 4, 23*
puss moth (poos môth) *p. 25*
red admiral butterfly (red ad′ mər əl
  but′ ər flī′) *p. 4*
silkworm (silk′ wurm′) *pp. 32, 33*
six-spot burnet moth (siks spot bər′ nət
  môth) *p. 22*
skipper butterfly (skip′ ər but′ ər flī′)
  pp. 20, 23

Pronunciation Key for Glossary

a   a as in **cat**, **bad**

ā   a as in **able**, ai as in **train**, ay as in **play**

ä   a as in **father**, **car**

e   e as in **bend**, **yet**

ē   e as in **me**, ee as in **feel**, ea as in **beat**, ie as in **piece**,
      y as in **heavy**

i   i as in **in**, **pig**

ī   i as in **ice**, **time**, ie as in **tie**, y as in **my**

o   o as in **top**

ō   o as in **old**, oa as in **goat**, ow as in **slow**, oe as in **toe**

ô   o as in **cloth**, au as in **caught**, aw as in **paw**, a as in **all**

oo   oo as in **good**, u as in **put**

o͞o   oo as in **tool**, ue as in **blue**

oi   oi as in **oil**, oy as in **toy**

ou   ou as in **out**, ow as in **plow**

u   u as in **up**, **gun**, o as in **other**

ur   ur as in **fur**, er as in **person**, ir as in **bird**,
      or as in **work**

yo͞o   u as in **use**, ew as in **few**

ə   a as in **again**, e as in **broken**, i as in **pencil**,
      o as in **attention**, u as in **surprise**

ch   ch as in **such**

ng   ng as in **sing**

sh   sh as in **shell**, **wish**

th   th as in **three**, **bath**

<u>th</u>   th as in **that**, **together**

GLOSSARY

These words are defined the way they are used in this book.

acid (as′ id) a substance that tastes sour, sharp, or biting

adapt (ə dapt′) to change to fit new conditions

alike (ə līk′) the same as; in the same way

ant (ant) a small insect that lives with others of its kind

antenna (an ten′ ə) one of two long, thin feelers on the heads of insects and some other animals *plural* **antennae**

antennae see **antenna**

apart (ə pärt′) away from one another

attack (ə tak′) to begin to fight against an enemy

body (bod′ ē) the whole of a person, animal, or plant

boiling (boi′ ling) in water the temperature 212° Fahrenheit, 100° Centigrade; hot enough to make liquid bubble

41

breathe (brēth) to take air into the
body and then force it back out

bush (boosh) a plant with many branches
that grows closer to the ground than a
tree does

butterfly (but′ ər flī′) an insect with a
thin body and four colored wings that
flies in the daytime

buzzing (buz′ ing) the humming sound bees
and some other insects make

cannot (kan′ ot *or* ka not′) is not able;
can not

case (kās) something used to hold or cover
a thing

caterpillar (kat′ ər pil′ ər) the wormlike
larva of a butterfly or moth

clothes (klōz *or* klōthz) things people
wear to cover their bodies

cloudy (klou′ dē) covered over with clouds

cocoon (kə koon′) a silky case spun by a
caterpillar

daytime (dā′ tīm′) the time when there is
light from the sun

dirty (dur′ tē) not clean; soiled

factory (fak′ tər ē) a building where things are made by machine

false (fôls) not real; used to trick or fool

female (fē′ māl) of the sex that has babies or produces eggs

form (fôrm) to take shape

furry (fur′ ē) having a covering of soft, thick hair

gather (ga<u>th</u>′ ər) to come or bring together in one place

grown (grōn) become as large as something is supposed to become

hatch (hach) to come from inside an egg

heat (hēt) warmth

hollow (hol′ ō) having an empty space inside

insect (in′ sekt) a small animal with a hard outer covering and without a backbone, such as a fly or ant, usually with six legs and two or four wings

itself (it self′) that same one

jaw (jô) the top or bottom hard mouthpart

of an animal or a person

juice (jo͞os) the liquid from fruits,
vegetables, and meats

larva (lär′ və) the wormlike form of an
insect after it hatches from an egg

leaf (lēf) one of the flat, green parts
that grow from a plant stem

life (līf) something plants and animals
have that lets them grow, develop, and
reproduce themselves

loose (lo͞os) able to move freely; not tight

lovely (luv′ lē) appearing pretty or
beautiful

male (māl) of the sex that can father
young

mate (māt) the male or female of a pair
of animals

migration (mī grā′ shən) a movement of a
number of living things from one place
to another

molting (mōlt′ ing) shedding hair, skin,
or feathers before growing a new covering

moth (môth) an insect that looks like a

butterfly but usually flies at night

mulberry (mul′ ber′ ē) a bush whose leaves
are the food of silkworms

nearby (nēr′ bī′) close; not far away

onto (ôn′ tōo *or* on′ tōo) to a place on
top or above

page (pāj) one of a book's paper sheets
on which words are printed

proboscis (prə bos′ əs) the sucking organ
of a butterfly or moth; a mouthpart

pupa (pyōo pə) the form of an insect after
it is a larva and before it becomes an
adult

reason (rē′ zən) a way to tell why
something happens

scale (skāl) one of many firm, flat parts
that covers the wings of a moth
or butterfly

season (sē′ zən) one of the four times of
the year — spring, summer, fall,
and winter

silk (silk) soft, shiny threads made by
some insects

silky (sil′ kē) looking or feeling like silk; smooth

skin (skin) the outer covering of the body

snake (snāk) an animal with a long body usually covered with scales and having no legs, arms, or wings

southern (su<u>th</u>′ ərn) toward the south

spin (spin) to twist fibers together to make thread

spiracle (spir′ i kəl) one of several holes in the body of an insect through which the insect breathes

split (split) to break into two or more parts

spool (spo͞ol) a small object shaped like a food can around which thread or cord can be wound

squirt (skwurt) to force out liquid in a narrow stream through a small opening

stem (stem) the main part of a plant that holds the leaves and flowers

sticky (stik′ ē) causing something to be held fast or unable to move easily

sting (sting) to wound with a sharp point

suck (suk) to draw something into the mouth

themselves (<u>th</u>em selvz′ *or* <u>th</u>əm selvz′)
the same ones

thirteen (thur′ tēn′) the number 13

thousand (thou′ zənd) the number 1,000

thread (thred) a long, thin cord

tongue (tung) the movable part in the mouth
used for tasting and swallowing

twisted (twist′ id) wound or turned around
something

waterweed (wô′tər wēd) a kind of plant
that grows in the water, like a water lily

wintertime (win′ tər tīm′) the time of the
year between fall and spring

wool (wool) cloth made from threads spun
from the hairs of sheep and some
other animals

Bibliography

Abisch, Roz. *Let's Find Out About Butterflies*.
New York: Franklin Watts, 1972.

Burton, Maurice, and Burton, Robert, editors.
The International Wildlife Encyclopedia.
20 vols. Milwaukee: Purnell Reference
Books, 1970.

Clarke, J. R. Gates. *A Golden Book of Butterflies*.
New York: Golden Press, 1963.

Hutchins, Ross E. *Scaly Wings: A Book About
Moths and Their Caterpillars*. New York:
Parents Magazine Press, 1971.

May, Julian. *Life Cycle of a Butterfly*.
Mankato, Minn.: Creative Educational Society,
1973.

Ridout, Ronald, and Holt, Michael. *Butterflies*.
New York: Grosset & Dunlap, 1974.